I hope you to all that you are looking for by investing in relationships

DF

SHOW UP!

Unlocking the Power of Relational Networking

DAVID FRANCE

Foreword by Toni Oloko

COPYRIGHT

Show Up: Unlocking the Power of Relational Networking

Published by David France

Cover art by Paul Kahn

The advice and strategies found within may not be suitable for every situation. This work is sold with the understanding that neither the author nor the publisher are held responsible for the results accrued from the advice in this book.

Printed in the United States of America
First Printing, November 2017
ISBN: 978-0-692-98363-8
www.DavidFranceViolin.com

"Show up when you say you will, and deliver what you say you will. These are the keys to unlocking the power in ANY relationship and David France nails it. If you only buy one book on relational networking, this is it."

-Paul C. Brunson World's #1 Matchmaker / TV Host Oprah Winfrey Network

'If you want to learn the art of Connecting with anyone and getting everything you want in life, David France has the answers. He is a real life expert, who teaches by genuinely walking the talk globally. I am blessed to have him in my network!'

-Pavlina Papalouka, Personal Branding Expert, Speaker, Coach

In business, in life, in health and family, you can't do it alone. David France brilliantly shows you how to build better and stronger relationships that will help you become the person you were always meant to be.

-Greg Rollett Emmy® Award Winning Producer, Founder, Ambitious.com

"Show up gives you the true meaning of life and how to get anything you want out of it. It gives you the secrets that I have been using to build teams, connect with influencers, and create events across the country. It holds the key to Success. Show up, and you will be amazed of the opportunities that will be presented to you."

**-Brandon T. Adams - Executive Producer / TV Host
of Ambitious Adventures**

Dedicated to Geraldine Williams (my grandmother)
From Barnes Ghaut, Nevis

CONTENTS

FOREWORD

By Toni Oloko

I FIRST MET David France in 2014 at an MIT networking event full of engineering PhDs. Given our lack of technical experience, neither of us had any business being there. I hid in the corner gorging on free snacks, observing David from afar, wondering how a black music teacher with an inner-city orchestra could captivate an Asian aquaponics professor with poor English. We struck up a conversation after the event, during which his genuine love of people became evident. To this day, he remains the best people-person I have ever met. That night I received the following email:

At 1:41 AM

"Great to meet you today at Co-Founders Day at MIT. Love your idea for Practice Gigs and wish you great success!! Hope you can make it to the Daniel Coyle event whenever that is scheduled. Also, I'll connect you with my friend that I was telling you about. Hey..have you ever heard of Youth Cities Mini Hack? You should go sometime and if you do, definitely connect with Vicky Wu who founded it. Here is a wonderful video that

Chelsea Clinton and NBC Nightly
News produced for my organization.

I hope our paths cross again!!"

-David

I was a high school student at the time with dreams of
starting a company, and he possessed what I most desired: the ability to instantaneously connect with people
at the most fundamental level of being.

I responded by asking to meet for coffee. He agreed. Just
a few sips in, he said, "I want to help you." Within 45
minutes, he taught me how to connect with anyone, how
to send a cold email, how to stay on the top of people's
mind, and how to network. Life moves faster around
David. We have been close friends ever since.

Using the skills I learned, I went on to build and sell a
company, raise venture capital, and have spoken around
the country — all before turning 20. My people skills
are what I get complimented on the most, all of which I
wholly owe to David.

To be honest, I was a bit sad when I discovered David
would be sharing his secrets with the world. But after
reading this book, I now see how the world will be made
richer by anyone who puts these ideas into practice. I
have no doubt that everyone holding this book can take

advantage of these tools. In this life-changing book, David illustrates what it means to be a giver rather than a taker, and reveals how to actionably turn everyday human interactions into meaningful opportunities.

Over the past three years, I have happily witnessed more people discover how truly remarkable of a person David is. Documentaries have been made about him, and people fly him around the world to speak, but he hasn't changed. He is still the same person that can chat with the homeless guy on the subway for an hour before meeting a billionaire. He is one of the few people with a genuine servant's heart who can also growth hack success.

You're holding an invaluable blueprint to networking without being transactional.

—Toni Oloko

INTRODUCTION

WHAT WILL BE your legacy? I've wrestled with this question for many years now. It is hard to know that one thing or those few things that will leave a lasting positive impact on our world. Currently, we are the most connected we've ever been while, at the same time, we're the hungriest we've ever been for meaningful relationships. Relationships can often be the missing key and the catalyst to help us realize our dreams. It's hard to know which single relationship or experience will be the most impactful. For instance, few would ever guess that a woman making Johnny cakes for her neighbors in the middle of the 20th century on the West Indian island of Nevis would later spark and inspire a world-class youth orchestra in Boston. This modest woman's selfless act would have a powerful domino effect, being the inspiration that led me to see the potent fruit of living generously by showing up and investing in relationships. Before diving into the meat of relationship-building, I'd love to tell you my story.

You can LEAVE the Bermuda Triangle!

A few years ago, I thought I had it made. I lived on the island of Bermuda and worked with amazing families, teaching their children to play the violin. An unbelievable chain of events would change the course of my life. The spark would be kindled by one simple yet powerful YouTube video. 40 years ago, in a parking garage in Caracas, Dr. Jose Antonio Abreu built a youth orchestra, against all odds, as a vehicle for social transformation. He believed that giving a kid an instrument, within the context of a supportive musical ensemble, could combat the feeling of isolation and promote youth development. I was in awe as I sat in front of the computer in Bermuda watching a sea of Venezuelan youth from some of their poorest neighborhoods performing in the world's great concert halls. I scoured the Internet for more videos and articles, often watching the same videos on repeat daily, when I stumbled upon a noble idea that resonated with my own personal beliefs. Music can not only be used as a mode of artistic expression, but also as a powerful vehicle for social transformation. I found what I had been looking for my entire life: I wanted to put my love for music at the intersection of educational disparities in our inner cities and create a hope-filled future for youth through the vehicle of an orchestra. A few years later, I was offered a full scholarship to study "music for social change" at the New England Conservatory of Music in Boston. The ability to make the move, from my dream job on a beautiful island to the life of a poor student, was built upon a few smaller but equally significant life-changing moments.

I was introduced to an original approach to the American Dream in John Piper's book, *Don't Waste Your Life* . His words, unmasking the American Dream as a lie, unhinged me from the ideals of getting rich quickly or using money for the sake of societal envy or whimsical ease. There have been so many scattered pieces to the puzzle that opened my eyes to the treasure found in relationships. The symbiotic give and take found in relationships is sweetened by being rich. "Consider Christ, he was rich, but he became poor so that he might make many rich."[1] The richer you are in wisdom, wealth or work ethic, the more you can give in a relationship and the more magnetic you appear to others. It is this magnetism that allows you to connect with influencers and other people you hope to do business with. I have found a foundation upon which I could build a cause and mutually beneficial relationships would be the key, connecting me to the resources I need.

My parents believed and risked everything to move to this country from a small island in the West Indies called Nevis. They had a firm belief that their born and unborn children could have a better life in a bigger country with more opportunities. My father grew up with his mother in a poor village called Barnes Ghaut. Every morning his mother would make delicious baked goods, like Johnny cakes, so that he could go through the village and give them to their neighbors. A few years ago, at my father's surprise birthday party, he recalled this story as the foundation and fuel for his own generosity. After moving to the United States, my parents worked more jobs than two people should be legally allowed, to ensure that their children could be whatever their dreams

---

1   The Bible, 2 Cor. 8:9

intimated. They showed up for work every day and still show up because they know that their dedication is creating a better future for their family and community. My parents have been giving their lives away for decades to our family, as well as to scores of immigrants needing a shoulder upon which to build THEIR American Dream.

Armed with a supportive family network, I started the violin at age 7 and faced a society which told me that the violin was not an instrument for black people. Overcoming this bias, I added over 10,000 hours of practice on the violin, experiencing a great deal along the way: great teachers, terrible teachers, free instruments, expensive instruments, extensive world travel, summer festivals, mistakes, life-changing performances and a childlike faith in possibility and the God behind opportunities. From my parents, I learned to dream big and to step out in faith. The journey toward starting the Roxbury Youth Orchestra has been full of amazing musical adventures, including performing with John Legend, Smokey Robinson, Quincy Jones, and being the Concertmaster of the first YouTube Symphony at Carnegie Hall.

I was rich! When the crowd told me that the violin was for white people, I showed up and found my own voice within its strings anyway; when people dismissed my aim to win an international competition, I showed up every night to a solitary room and practiced as if my life depended on it. Eventually winning the YouTube Symphony competition. I didn't have material wealth, but was blessed with the experiences and skills that come from showing up, over time. I put my nose to the grindstone, met people that didn't want to meet me, and consistently reached toward the stars, even in the face of my own doubt. The generous spirit that moved through my grandmother Geraldine Williams, who showed up by waking up early every morning and making Johnny cakes for her neighbors, also moved through my father who out of kindness, housed more people than should fit in a small house. These examples would later inspire me to show up and give my life away to underserved youth in inner city Boston.

Thank you TED Prize

The videos of the Simon Bolivar Youth Orchestra in Venezuela led me to the TED Prize video of Dr. José Antonio Abreu, Founder of El Sistema. This famous conference hosting the brightest minds on our planet, annually awards a TED Prize to select individuals whose "wish to change the world" is then funded. Dr. Abreu was awarded the prize in 2009 and "wished" to start a training program that selected 10 people from around the world each year to train in Boston and Venezuela, so as to bring El Sistema to the United States. I was shocked to win this fellowship in 2011 and began the journey of following my dream to see the work in Venezuela for myself and use that vision to start my own orchestra.

During my last week in Venezuela, we pulled up in a small village in the city of Coro called Las Panelas. We were told that, if we were going to volunteer in that community, we would have to leave before sundown because it was a dangerous neighborhood. The project in Las Panelas was started by Isandra Campos. A year before we arrived, Isandra, a mother of 5, moved out of her home and in with her own mother so that the neighborhood children could use her home as a daily haven to make music. Seven days a week, neighborhood kids pour in and out of her home singing in a choir and playing various instruments. The music flooding out of the house is the curiosity of the neighbors as they sit on their porches and listen. Every day we saw children peeking through open windows inspired by the music. Isandra's spirit of generosity stopped me in my tracks. In the backyard, she raised chickens and sold their eggs for one Bolivar each then, with the money she earned, bought the music for the kids. What Isandra receives from this investment is far more than she has given up and she is still there to this day. Because she has consistently shown up on behalf of forgotten youth, the life trajectory of these kids will be forever changed. This is the fruit of her joyful sacrifice. I realized that I no longer had any excuses in my mission to starting a similar orchestra. The question, however, remained: for which community would I move out of my house and sell eggs?

After a few months in Venezuela, I returned to Boston where I fell in love with the community of Roxbury. Growing up, many would say to me, "I've never met a black person that played the violin," and I'd usually respond, "Me neither!" I was excited to develop a world-class youth orchestra in what has been dubbed "the most important black community in New England."

After graduating from the New England Conservatory, I subleased my apartment and spent the next half-year sleeping on couches and concrete while devoting my afternoons to forming strategic relationships to build the Roxbury Youth Orchestra. In February of 2013, the Roxbury Youth Orchestra was launched from its new home in the auditorium of Dearborn Middle School. Six weeks after our launch, NBC News sent a film crew and their famous correspondent Chelsea Clinton to cover the story. One minute after the story aired, I was asked to tell my story at a national conference. We started with the obstacle of no money, so I was forced to find a way over this seemingly dream-ending barrier. The foundation I built was a sea of relationships, nurtured through the art of showing up around the city, empowering the people that also showed up, and allowing them to invest in my dream.

Our orchestra is now a safe house for youth and youth development in the community of Roxbury. It is a furnace for musical excellence and community renewal. An orchestra is a model community where members must listen to each other and work together to achieve success. I call my umbrella organization 'Revolution of Hope'. This revolution is envisioned as a cathartic social movement that changes the face of institutions and can bring a liberating freedom to pursue dreams that were not possible before. The goal is not merely to give kids a place to go, but to show them how to build a home. We strive to create a lasting community upon a tradition of equity, opportunity and confidence that comes from music. Our academic goals fit alongside our social goals, as we believe that an excellent, joy-filled music program can affect executive function skills and teach 21st century workforce skills. Ideally, after our time together, our students can feel empowered to walk onto the streets of Boston, armed with self-esteem and the will to dream.

A few summers ago, I arrived in Chicago with just enough money to take the subway into the city. While there, I proceeded to busk, performing in the subway system. I'm never a fan of the police but one night, while illegally busking in the subway, I was "caught". Two armed officers stopped me and asked for my permit. My heart was racing. I stopped playing and began rustling through my case, taking out extra strings, books, computers, papers, music, pencil shavings, and then finally my newly purchased Boston subway permit. I placed it sideways on my case and pointed to it. They kindly said, "Just keep it visible; you sound great." As they walked away, I started to play "Somewhere over the Rainbow". In the distance, I heard a very low voice singing. When the man came near I noticed that the man who sang had a cane and was blind. He stood directly in front of me and we continued our soulful version of the song. It was so incredibly moving that I had goose bumps. Standing next to us was a random guy with his jaw dropping. After we finished, he reached for some change and threw it in. He then reached for more change, then a few dollars, then threw all his money in the case, saying he was so moved. The blind man said he had nothing to give but I disagreed. The experience of performing with him was priceless.

I sincerely believe that it is only when we give our lives away that we truly begin to live. We give our lives away by showing up not only at events but also by being present in a conversation, coming early to an event to help set up, staying late to take down, giving advice, listening and with a myriad of other ways we can add value to others. Powerful relationships have a special magic when one or both parties give more than they expect back in return. When the gifting of ourselves happens in simple authentic ways, this creates a natural atmosphere for powerful relationships, which are best nurtured when, over time, we: Show up!

MISSION

The ideas in this book emerge from the fruits of my own personal story. I don't believe that ideas exist in a vacuum but rather they find their genesis in the soils of our unique narratives. I'm fascinated by the fact that a group of people raised in the same environment, often in the same family or community, can routinely turn out so differently. My search for the common denominator in so many of my unbelievable opportunities has led me to the conclusion that meaningful relationships and consistently showing up are the keys to unlocking a lifetime of opportunities. When others make excuses to stay at home or believe that an opportunity is out of their reach, showing up and investing in the relationships that present themselves, has for me, made all the difference.

This book explores the connection between relationships and generosity, giving you actionable strategies to help you stand out from the crowd and connect with the people perfect for you. Along the way, through stories and ideas, you will gain tools to help you nurture mutually beneficial relationships.

Chapter
1

Silas Hagerty

WHEN I LIVED on the island of Bermuda I often traveled to New York City. It was one of the few gateway cities in the United States you could travel to from the island. After numerous trips, I finally accepted the fact that I HATED the city. Being lost amongst Times Square revelers, walking aimlessly through the corridor of buildings, was not quite what I was looking for. I wasn't interested in Broadway, I never truly felt at home at museums, I had no interest in seeing the Yankees and there are only so many times you can walk across the Brooklyn Bridge. When Island Fever sets in and you need to get off the rock, New York was the cheapest option. A wise friend once told me, "Wherever you go, there you are," and, over time, I realized that New York wasn't the problem, I was the problem. My intersection with the city was unfocused. I took inventory of the things I loved and began to dream of ways to explore some of them in New York.

I've always loved movies ever since I was a kid and watched more than my fair share. I began to wonder why I'd never imagined exploring the film industry of the city, so I resolved to dig around the Internet and find a film company I could help. I'm the type of person that enjoys just being a fly on the wall in a chic room. I don't need to be the center of attention; just a small cog in a magnificent machine. I became a bit overwhelmed by the enormity of the city's film industry and was at a loss with knowing where to begin or who I should even contact.

One night, I received a message from the founder of the travel website couchsurfing.com. He shared a short film that his buddy had made about how the sport of soccer was being used in Lusaka to help fight the spread of AIDS. Looking back at this moment, it probably wasn't too ethical for the founder to spam his users inbox to promote his friend's film, but I'm glad he did. I watched the film and was impressed. The filmmaker also had a profile on couchsurfing.com and, with some digging, I found out that he was based in New York. I immediately sent him a message asking if I could be his intern, then waited in eager anticipation.

A few days later I received a response, a phone number and a request asking me to call him. I jumped at this opportunity and, before the month was over, I was on a phone call with a real live documentary filmmaker. It was funny because he was just as excited as I was and just as uncertain of our next steps. After the call, only two things were certain; one, that I was going to be his very first intern and, two, that this guy was probably the coolest person I'd ever met. For hours we traded stories from our lives couched in the philosophies that enabled our decisions. The details of my internship were not clear but we both sensed that it would be a blast to work together. I bought a ticket to New York and, a few months later, showed up at Silas's Brooklyn apartment.

When I arrived, Silas opened the door and I was welcomed in by a bright-eyed filmmaker with a huge smile. I was ready to do anything, even wash the dishes if it would give this young filmmaker more time to make movies. I walked in thinking, *let's get to work!* but instead he said, "Let's go to the roof, there's a great view there." A great view? I was confused but I went along with it. I wanted to work, but he wanted to chat on the roof. The conversation on the roof was more electric than our previous phone conversations and the Manhattan skyline made it even more epic. When we returned to his apartment, he taught me the tedious job of entering his film into film festivals. I sunk my teeth into this task while he went back to editing videos. This wasn't a fancy Hollywood studio; this was his kitchen and he sat a few feet away from me at his computer. Every few minutes we couldn't help but revive the memorable conversation from the roof. I went there for an internship and I was wondering if maybe I had found a friend.

After the weeklong project, he told me that he had over 500 unopened emails that he received when his documentary was published on couchsurfing.com. I volunteered to be his ghostwriter and respond to them as him.

I didn't want the relationship to end. I couldn't just say goodbye to someone who shared a similar passion for travel, film and people. He agreed and, over the next few months, I became Silas Hagerty.

Two years later, when Silas was editing his first feature-length documentary, he decided I'd be ideal for the soundtrack. He flew me in from Bermuda, locked me in a basement and, two days later, my violin was soaring through some of the most powerful scenes of his movie. If you told me 10 years ago that interning for an unknown filmmaker in Brooklyn would lead to performing at his wedding, being featured on the soundtrack of an incredible documentary and launching a film school in Maine, plus that I would be in a short film with Ethan Hawke, I never would have believed you. But these accolades have been the least significant fruit of knowing Silas Hagerty. When I met him, all I wanted to do was to wash his dishes, but over the years he's become my friend. He's challenged me to see that networking isn't about what you can get from others, but instead about how you can use your gifts to make a positive impact in the world. In the process of giving, you will receive more than you could have thought to ask. Knowing Silas has been an epic ride and, even though our collective resume is impressive, I'd still show up in Maine and wash his dishes any day.

CHAPTER
2

HOW TO BUILD AUTHENTIC RELATIONSHIPS

I CONSIDER THIS book to be a resource of tools that, over the years, have led me to some impressive outcomes. So, let's now assemble a toolbox of tips and tricks that will serve as your launching pad for building significant relationships. This is just a starter pack to which you will add your own nuanced ideas that will be tailored to your unique personality and needs.

Authenticity

The number one way to form lifelong meaningful connections is through a method we've been told our entire lives: *Just be yourself.* Clichéd catchphrases can easily become background noise, undecipherable in the landscape of mantras. So, let's take a moment to unpack this idea with a few revealing questions.

Who are you when disconnected from your professional identity? Take a few minutes and answer the following:

- What is one thing you want to accomplish before you die that is not connected to a career or professional goal?
- What are two SEEMINGLY contrasting words that would give someone a more nuanced view into your character? (e.g. selfish and generous)
- What gives your life meaning?
- What have you most recently complained about regarding another person's actions, personally or professionally?
- What is your greatest fear?
- What have been the biggest obstacles in your life up to this point?

The more you know about yourself and your own needs, the better you can deeply connect with others. Sharing our dreams outside of our careers can be a subtle way to begin a more nuanced professional relationship. Authenticity is rarely two-dimensional and, when we only allow people to see us from the lens of our resume personified, we may be losing an opportunity to create a memorable first impression.

The questions above should be a springboard for you to dream up your own questions that will help shape how you think about yourself. We are constantly being pressured to fit into simplified boxes, but truly knowing ourselves involves the ability to see the thin layers of differences that populate the atmosphere of our character.

Your biggest obstacle may be your greatest advantage. The most interesting people I've ever met are always in a state of becoming. How do you know if an organism is alive? It metabolizes food, it responds to stimuli and it's GROWING! Knowing yourself includes understanding your unique needs. Look at your answer to the question:

What have you most recently complained about regarding another person's actions, personally or professionally?

We all have different pressure points. When someone pushes the wrong button, or gives us service that isn't ideal, our response isn't limited to a knee-jerk reaction. Rather than resort to criticizing, we can redirect the complaint into a resolve to treat others in a better way. The more we look inward when conditions out of our control bother us, our response has the potential for greater impact. I believe that our happiness is directly related to the degree to which we think outside of ourselves. If you are unsure of what you might do, just look inside and study your own personal longings then gift those away to others. If what you give away comes from a personal place of need, it may have a profound effect on others. You could say this is a twist on the 'golden rule' of treating others the way we want to be treated.

So many people want to meet that billionaire that will write them a million-dollar check. The truth is that, if you are ever given that check, you will eventually need another one. An authentic connection, where you resolve to generously add value over time, has more benefits than a 'one-night stand'.

Natural Connections

Understanding yourself in a more complex way is the bridge to the second strategy in our toolbox: *Natural Connections*. When at a networking event, the most comfortable people to talk to are those that you get along with the easiest. This can happen between people with a broad range of similarities. A natural connection happens when both parties form a mutually beneficial bond to any degree, just by being themselves. You may be severely limiting yourself if you only restrict yourself to meeting people who are in your professional industry. It can be tempting to write people off if they don't seem to fit an immediate need. Some of the ways people connect naturally include:

1. Sports
2. Values / Ideology
3. Hobbies
4. Family background
5. Language
6. Music

This is by no means an exhaustive list and you will certainly come up with your own ideas. You might now be wondering about the people with whom a connection might not seem . We live in an increasingly fragmenting world and it's been a personal joy to pursue meaning-ful connections with people that aren't exactly like me. Usually these connections are based on our similar val-ues. Getting to a point in a conversation where values are uncovered is much trickier, but I'll give a few strat-egies to lead you to these answers in the next section.

CHAPTER

3

STRATEGIES FOR BUILDING AUTHENTIC RELATIONSHIPS

Listen

PEOPLE ENJOY TALKING about themselves and, if asked a series of thoughtful questions, may become open to a deeply meaningful first conversation. This leads us to our next tool: Active Listening.

Professional relationship-building skills are not much different from the behaviors that would make you attractive at a cocktail party. When you decide to focus on listening to a conversation, the focus is no longer on you. This gives you room to ask clarifying questions that may lead to more meaningful answers. When you ask thoughtful questions, the person in your presence feels valued. It is important to also gauge the comfort level of the other person to determine where to draw the line with questioning.

Add Value

When you listen with the intent of asking meaningful questions, you will hear ways that you can be valuable to someone's business or life goals. Listening with this goal helps us to be more attentive during our interactions. A few questions that can help you see where you can best add value are:

1. What are they passionate about?

2. What are some of their current needs?

3. What are their goals in the next few months?

4. What are they struggling with?

5. What types of people are they hoping to meet?

6. What are some of their mundane tasks that can be done by someone else?

If given the pleasure of working on a project, I always try to under-promise and over-deliver. I am careful not to undertake a project that is too burdensome and won't allow me the time to give more value than I've promised. The most indispensable members of the community are those who provide the most value. It is easy to make promises but much harder to deliver on them. If we all committed to making less promises and delivering more value, more ideas would thrive, and communities would become stronger forces for good in our world.

I love asking people about their dreams outside of their profession. If someone in my network can help them realize this dream, I'll gladly make the introduction. Too often we only allow ourselves to understand our business relationships through only one funnel. Caring to ask about their dreams and aligning your work with them can add an individualized touch to our connections. Knowing these dreams broadens the spectrum by which we can make an impact on someone's life.

Community is most powerful when the members don't sit around waiting to be served but use their resources for the benefit of each other. If no one reaches out to you, then you have the honor of being the one extending your hand in the form of your unique resources.

Brandon T. Adams

If you told me three years ago that a viral video of a drunk college student demanding jalapeño bacon mac and cheese would lead to me becoming an Associate Producer of an Emmy nominated TV show, I would never have believed you. I didn't even know jalapeño bacon mac and cheese existed and the viral video was far from positive. Before the video ends, the college student assaults the cafeteria worker and is carted off by the police. While the video was floating around the Internet, some of my friends gathered for our weekly outing for 30-cent chicken wings. The conversation drifted to the video. We had all seen the video and, before long, this group of entrepreneurs started brainstorming ways to turn this humiliating video into a force for good. Our conversation lasted until the early hours of the next day and, before we parted ways, the Jalapeño Bacon Mac and Cheese crowdfunding campaign was born. The Internet coughed up the university's original recipe and we devised a strategy to feed this dish to 100 homeless people in Boston. The campaign was wildly successful, raising over $5,000 to feed 100 people living on the streets and to outfit an entire shelter with winter gear.

While updating the project page on Indiegogo, I stumbled upon another campaign for a new conference called The Young Entrepreneur Convention. The campaign was electric and casted a vision for bringing together millennial entrepreneurs with a passion to change the world. In a single page, their team communicated their ideals and values, getting me fired up to get involved. I reached out to the founder asking if I could help, but didn't hear back. After a series of follow-up emails over the next few weeks, I received a short reply.

Hey David!

What value can you bring to the convention? What's your proposal? Thanks for being persistent. I appreciate that :)

Brandon

This email took me by surprise. I believed in the principal of adding value to the people you meet but no one had ever asked me this question so directly. My respect for this team grew even more. They had an unwavering commitment to creating the best young entrepreneurship conference in the country and realized that not every offer to help would be a perfect match. I again poured through their campaign and website re-igniting my longing to be involved. A few hours later, I sent this answer:

Brandon,

Thanks for getting back to me. I love this project. Value? I bring passion, tenacity and a roll up your sleeves spirit to everything I do. I have connections to incredible speakers through a few different networks. This year I won Top 40 Urban Innovators Under 40 in the United States. I have a lot of connections to great speakers. As an African American, I bring diversity and, as a former expatriate, I bring nuanced perspectives. I have also spoken at a number of conferences, usually receiving the only standing ovation of the entire conference. Although I've been in *Time magazine*, *CNN, NBC, Al Jazeera*, won YouTube's first international competition, and am featured in two documentaries, I'm not too proud to sweep the floors for causes I believe in... you won't often find that kind of value at your door...

Brandon agreed to bring me on board as a volunteer and a few months later, I was in Iowa. I arrived a week before the conference to help Brandon in any way possible. I was willing to do anything, and my first job was to set up 700 chairs for the convention. This wasn't the most glamorous role, but I knew that being there to help with the tasks that no one else wanted would give Brandon's team the freedom to focus on the more crucial details of the weekend. Adding value, in small but significant ways, can be the foundation that sparks a more involved relationship. A year later, I was assigned my own event during the convention and later that year Brandon asked me to become the Associate Producer of the Emmy-nominated show Ambitious Adventures. Showing up with a sincere willingness to add value to someone else and then using that opportunity to forge a relationship, can become the vehicle for inconceivable future advantages.

Strategies for Building Authentic Relationships: Study the Person You Will Be Meeting

If you know in advance who will be in the room at a networking event or a conference, it can be helpful to do some background research on the attendees or speakers. One of the easiest ways to know who will be attending a conference is to see who is using the conference hashtags or commenting on the event's social media page. You can learn more about the attendees via their LinkedIn profiles, Twitter accounts, websites, and various other channels. The people who are savvy enough to make themselves known before an event might just be the types of people you are hoping to meet. You want to also be this person, because there will be people using this approach and looking for you. Making an intelligent comment on an online post is an effective way to start a dialogue. Depending on how the interaction grows, you may want to schedule coffee during one of the breaks at the event to chat in person. This approach is particularly helpful at large events, where the number of people can be intimidating.

I had the honor of speaking at HubSpot's conference Inbound 2017 recently where one of the attendees created the hashtag #BlackatInbound, looking to build a community of African Americans in the industry of inbound marketing. The originator of the hashtag was asked by the conference to actively help promote the African American speakers and to promote informal networking opportunities. In a conference boasting over 21,000 people, this approach helped to create a community within a community. It was powerful to see how something as simple as a hashtag could help a group feel a sense of belonging and connect people who may have never met.

Ask Advice Then Do What You're Told

There are numerous strategies for building authentic relationships and this list is by no means exhaustive. The last strategy I'll present is: *Ask for advice, then do what you're told.*

One of the best ways to begin to form a significant connection with a speaker at an event is to ask for their advice. Why would a busy person of influence ever take the time to get to know you? When most people stand in line to meet a keynote speaker, they usually ask for the gratuitous selfie or else shower the speaker with praise. Those who are strategic about creating a tribe of powerful connections seek to create a more lasting impression, by trying to find unique ways to stand out. Asking the right question can be the key to getting into the speaker's inner circle.

One of the best questions you can ask a speaker is a burning question you've been struggling with, which is also in line with their expertise. When you are given advice, ask if you could send them a follow-up. If you ask an intelligent and short question that excites an answer, you can create a more memorable encounter than with the person before you who took the selfie. If the speaker is willing to give you the time to think through your obstacle, this can trigger them into caring about the work you are doing.

It's also possible that the speaker may be excited to answer your question, but the length of the line makes thinking of an answer impractical. In that case, you can ask if they wouldn't mind if you sent the question in an email. If they agree and then send you an answer to your burning question, the relationship is more likely to mature. The next step will be sending a follow-up, detailing how you implemented their advice. Doing what you're told shows not only flexibility but a willingness to continue growing. If you decide that their advice might not work in your situation, send a note thanking them for their time and briefly relate how you pivoted from their idea. Gratitude, along with showing your thought process, is an effective way to stand out and begin a relationship with an influencer.

Sean Gardner

There isn't much that can separate me from a home-cooked meal involving chicken. But one Saturday, a few years ago, a friend of mine called me from an event just before I put the chicken cordon bleu I had prepared in the oven. I was trying a new recipe, so his call wasn't completely convenient. He is a voracious networker so to this day, when I see his name pop up on my phone, I answer it. He told me that he was at a Harvard Business School happy hour with Forbes' No.1 social media influencer.

That title sounded impressive but, after a long week, my chicken cordon bleu was more appealing. He made every attempt to convince me to make the bike ride over to Harvard Square, but I resisted. As he continued, I decided to consult Google for the name Sean Gardner. LinkedIn didn't reveal too many more accolades, but one minor detail stuck out to me – Sean Gardner was black.

"You didn't tell me he was BLACK!!!"

The previous accolades did impress me and I was, at the time, curious to figure out how to wade through the noise on Twitter. When I saw that he was black, however, I thought this might be a factor that could persuade him to 'help a brotha out' who had a similar interest in social media.

I rode to Harvard Square in record time and, when I arrived, Sean was talking to a group of business school students, who were clinging to his every word. My friend was at a table behind him, also in complete admiration. We eagerly listened to his conversation from behind and eventually he turned around and said hello, asking what brought us to the event. My friend came to the event as a volunteer and, after his answer, Sean turned to me.

"Sir, 20 minutes ago I was about to put my chicken cordon bleu in the oven and my friend here demanded I come meet the Forbes No.1 social media influencer. I realized the chicken would have to wait and I biked faster than I've ever ridden in my entire life to get here... nice to meet you."

After that introduction, Sean turned his back to the group with whom he sat and gave us 30 minutes of his undivided attention. He detailed his strategy of how he built his following on Twitter and challenged us to do the same. I had nothing to lose, with only 440 followers on Twitter, so Sean had just given us a goldmine of information. We decided to precisely follow his advice and, two years later, I had amassed over 23,000 followers. In the years following our meeting, I added a few ideas of my own to his method and, three years later, I was invited to do a social media workshop of my own at a national conference.

Sean gave us his email to follow up and I was able to thank him, describing how I executed on his approach. Since then, Sean has quietly followed and engaged with my work and I believe this is only the beginning of this story. Powerful relationships are not about what you can get from someone at that moment, but enjoying the rewards of a lifelong connection. Giving an influencer an opportunity to see how you work through a set of directives shows how you respond to new information. This depth of knowledge can build a foundation of trust over time.

CHAPTER

4

HOW TO MEET PEOPLE: SHOW UP

NOW THAT WE'VE talked about how to build relationships, let's talk about **how to meet people**. My No.1 mantra for meeting new people is to simply *Show Up!* Consistently showing up to events in Boston, as well as around the country and the world, has led me to some exceptionally productive relationships and a few mind-blowing opportunities. The number of people who are surprised when I show up for events that I've committed to attending, has been shocking. In our modern world, we've become accustomed to people not following through on their promises and have even come to expect it. The regrettable outcome happens when we give ourselves permission to become sloppy with our commitments. Of course, situations arise that are out of our control and we may find ourselves busier than we first assumed – but this is not what I'm describing.

For some, it has become commonplace to make promises to show up as a form of courtesy. We fear offending our colleagues by saying no if we have no intention of showing up. We justify our response because, in the back of our minds, there's a small chance we may be there.

The fear of missing out (FOMO) also plays a significant role in this phenomenon. Social media has increased our awareness of what is happening in our community, while also widening our lens into the social lives of our network. When time is perceived as scarce, the pressure can mount to decide what to prioritize. Then, when a better option comes along, our commitments are sacrificed at the altar of alternatives.

Showing up becomes considerably more impressive in a culture that expects you not to follow through on your word. This isn't the century's worst crime, but not showing up can definitely limit your opportunities. We have all heard that the extremely successful have failed more often than most have ever tried. This holds true with opportunity. The seemingly lucky have not only outperformed most people, but also show up more often.

Show Up: Networking Events

If you attend events within your field and outside of your vocation, then you will meet a wider variety of people. Having a broader spectrum of influences can have a profound effect on how we look at ourselves and the world. I used to think that 'networking' was a dirty word that involved meeting people with the primary goal of using them for my own benefit. In the age of Tinder and the "swipe right" mentality, we are being programmed to judge books by their cover, putting people into restrictive boxes. We can wrongly think things like "I'm an entrepreneur, but she's a doctor, so she has nothing to offer me."

The first time I attended a networking event in Boston, my goal was to listen to the stories of as many people as possible, while keeping my own career hidden. Having this goal allowed me to spend my time trying to discover what questions I could ask to gain a more nuanced picture of the person in front of me. Every Thursday in Boston I attend a networking event called The Venture Café. It's a weekly gathering in Cambridge that is one of the pillars of Boston's entrepreneurial ecosystem. They believe there is enormous value found in relationships and that the nonnegotiable variable in any relationship is time. They trust that providing a reliable weekly "watering hole" for spontaneous interactions will, over time, cause relationships and collaborations to grow. When you consistently show up, not only are you building these relationships, but you are also exponentially increasing your chances of crossing paths with opportunities that may, to an outsider, appear to be a stroke of luck. I don't believe in luck, but I've adopted the axiom that luck is the intersection where preparation meets opportunity. Showing up consistently increases your potential "opportunity" and the converse may put limits on your apparent "luck".

I recently read that "as long as you don't give up, failure is just progress in disguise." When you show up regularly, it is inevitable that you will go to many events where you won't naturally connect with anyone. I am motivated to push through these less than ideal times because of the growing list of remarkable sequences of events that have come about when I've "shown up" even when conditions were less than ideal.

Adrian Lipscombe

As you now know, one of my weekly traditions is attending Boston's Venture Café networking event. One beautiful summer afternoon, a few years ago, every excuse came to mind to skip it, in favor of a long bike ride. I silently encouraged myself to "just SHOW UP." I hopped on my bike and headed over to the event, intending to go through the motions of meeting people. While there, I was cornered into a conversation. The kind and very enthusiastic gentleman visiting from Chattanooga, Tennessee told me about the growing entrepreneurial scene there. As he spoke, I couldn't imagine how anything he said related to me but, over time, his passion for his city intrigued me more and more. He then told me that the city was having a contest to form an international delegation of influencers to advise the city. This group of 10 people, from around the world, would be given an all-expense paid insider's look into the city's ecosystem and get a chance to advise the city in its move toward becoming a national hub for early stage start-ups.

Before the conversation ended, he asked me to apply to the delegation. I thought, what part of 'I'm a violinist' did he not understand? Why would he even ask me to consider this? No clear answer came to mind but I decided to apply. I've come to believe that, whenever possible, I should apply to whatever I am offered because sometimes my colleagues may have a better idea of my chances of success than I do. I also never assume that anything I am offered will ever be offered again.

After applying, I quickly forgot about Chattanooga and this so-called delegation. A month later, out of the blue, I receive an email invitation to be a part of the Waypaver Delegation. I was honored to be invited to this brain trust. I never imagined an acceptance scenario in my wildest dreams. A few weeks later, I was in Chattanooga and there met nine of the most impressive young people I have ever encountered. Among them was Adrian Lipscombe, an architect, city planner, bike enthusiast and restaurateur. It made sense to me that she was a part of the delegation based on her incredible accolades, but my participation still baffled me. At this point that didn't matter anymore; I showed up and was now a part of an incredible tribe.

The team spent long days wrestling through big ideas with the city's innovation community and with each other. Over the course of the week, I became close friends with Adrian and, on our last night, she told me about an award she recently won. She was named one of the top 40 urban innovators under the age of 40 in the United States, known as the Vanguard Fellowship. She urged me to apply. I didn't see what she saw in me, but I had learned an important lesson. The last time when I persevered and did what I was told, in the face of doubt, I ended up a member of an international delegation. A year later, I applied and, shortly afterward, found out that I too had won a Vanguard Fellowship, naming me as one of the Top 40 Urban Innovators Under 40. It has become clear that, if I didn't show up to the Venture Café that hot uninspiring day in August, none of these incredible opportunities would have happened. That day, my body followed my feet, causing me to show up and leading me to numerous opportunities that have given me prestigious accolades, new friendships and, together, has changed how I see and interact with the world.

How to Meet People: Be a Connector

There are numerous types of people that you will find at an event. One of the most magnetic groups in the room are the connectors. These are people who leverage their networks for the benefit of others. The best connectors realize that everyone they meet can be a possible resource for someone currently in their life or someone they may meet in the future. Listening is one of their key strategies and the conversation is valued regardless of whether or not the person has an immediate perceived value.

If you consistently make connections on behalf of others, more and more people, over time, start networking for

YOUR benefit! This has been a mind-blowing discovery. If everyone in the world is removed by only by six degrees of separation, the more connectors you know, the smaller the world becomes. Connectors are often attracted to each other because of similar attitudes toward meeting new people. There are so few people who genuinely look out for others, therefore, when connectors meet, there can be an instant connection. Some of the most dynamic business relationships are between a group of authentic connectors and the fruit of these relationships benefit countless others, while providing real value for the connectors themselves. Networking with connectors and becoming one yourself can help you to meet the people you've always dreamed of meeting. Be certain to always be aware of your motives, however, because the best connectors can sniff out insincerity.

Harvard

One morning I received an email, out of the blue, inviting me to speak at an event in Roanoke, Virginia. I immediately called the number in the message, responding "YES! What's the question?" I was quite curious as to how they had discovered me and their answer took me by surprise. Anita, the founder of CityWorks Xpo, had watched a speech I had given that I did not even know was online. The wildest part of the story is what she could not see in the video; there was no one in the audience, besides the camera guy. The conference placed the talk online and, a year later, I was being invited to Virginia. Two weeks later, with an e-ticket loaded on my phone, I showed up to the airport. But there was a major problem. The wrong name had been placed on the ticket. I never look at the e-ticket confirmations I receive to see if my name is correctly listed; I just assume that it is. I frantically made numerous unanswered calls to Virginia to get the ticket resolved. Over the next four hours, while standing at the ticket counter, I exhausted every possible option I could imagine to fix the problem. The night would end with my worst nightmare. My phone calls and texts were never returned, and I instead returned to my apartment in Boston.

Early the next morning, my phone rings and the voice on the other end of the line had clearly been crying. It was Anita. While fighting back tears, she told me how she had misplaced her cell phone the previous night and missed all my messages. She apologized profusely and then asked me if I still wanted to come to Virginia. She was prepared to buy me another ticket.

> *"My bags are still packed,*
> *YES, I'd love to come!"*

An hour later, I was at Logan Airport and on my way to Virginia. I arrived, gave my prepared speech and was then ushered back to the airport. The next day I received another email from Anita. Two women from Harvard University were in the audience and, to my amazement, they wanted ME to come and speak there in 2 weeks! Again, my answer was 'YES! What's the question!?'

Since this experience, I've had the honor of speaking at Harvard five times and this also opened the door to speak at MIT. I often think back to that speech I gave to an empty room. If I didn't show up and give the talk of my life to that empty room, I never would have been invited to Virginia. If my plane ticket fiasco caused me to lose interest in going to Virginia or if I thought there was no value in flying to a small city for less than 24 hours, I never would have spoken at Harvard and MIT.

The art of simply showing up can become the foundation for many of our most impressive opportunities. We never know, however, which seemingly insignificant opportunity will lead to something bigger, therefore, we should treat every opportunity in front of us as if it is a chance of a lifetime. Even if it doesn't lead to something more impressive, your character and work ethic will be impacted, and you will become known as someone who treats everyone and every opportunity with dignity, respect and importance. "Wherever you go, there you are"; becoming a classier human is a far worthier accolade than any single professional pursuit. Your character and vibe are the magnets that attract your tribe. Mind what you're attracting.

How to Meet People: The Pursued

There is a category of people that I describe as, '*those who want to be found.*' Up to this point, we've only talked about the art of meeting people from the seeker's perspective. Now we'll take a moment to turn the tables and look at the *pursued*.

Have you ever thought about why you want to build your professional network? The more you can analyze your personal motivation, the better you will understand those you hope to meet. Who do you want to meet and why? What are your professional needs? What value can you add to those you hope to meet?

Now imagine this: You are not alone. We've all heard that the social media space is an overcrowded cocktail party. One of the main reasons people feel overwhelmed by it is because their main goal is to have THEIR voice heard in the myriad of voices. Let's step back for a minute and change our perspective. Could it be that we are so overwhelmed with the idea of social media because we are looking at it in the wrong way? What if we spend more time *listening* rather than trying to be heard? What if those you want to meet WANT to be found? They have been trying to get your attention all along but maybe we have been talking past each other.

When we turn the table in this direction, it becomes clear that the noisy social media space is our oyster. The missing key to the equation: listening. The answer has been in our faces the entire time, but our own agendas have blurred this truth.

Have you ever written a reporter, magazine, blog writer, influencer, or anyone else from your list of dream contacts and not received a response? Why don't we hear from the leaders in our field? One reason might be because you are one of many vying for their attention. In the future section of this book entitled *How to write a cold call email*, we will talk about how to make a powerful first impression, but now let's flip the script a bit.

The strategy to connect with those who want to be found is simple yet time-intensive. Let's dive straight into the method I've discovered. First, find newcomers in various industries who are trying to build a tribe for their work. In every field, there are people doing exceptional work without much fanfare or media attention. One of the places I often look for undiscovered talent is crowdfunding campaigns. A well-designed campaign will give you a sense of the team's vision and future potential. Spending the time to study their work and looking for common denominators will help determine whether your work might creatively align with their goals. If it's a match, reach out. Gary Vaynerchuk may never feature you on his vlog but Brandon T. Adams might. Here are a few industries in which to look for newcomers:

1. Magazines

2. Tech

3. Authors

4. Bloggers / Vloggers

5. Food & Beverage

6. YouTubers / Actors

7. Musicians

8. Podcasters

Once you have come up with your list of influencer genres, ask yourself what channels are they using to get your attention? They might be using a Kickstarter campaign, Facebook groups, local meetups, booths at conferences, sponsors for events, videos or other platforms. When you have determined these avenues, start listening to learn their values, work ethic and other unique offerings and needs. Read their blogs, write intelligent responses and, in time, you will begin to get their attention. Anyone posting content is looking for engagement. When you give them this attention they will start noticing YOU.

One of the best times to get on board an incredible project is at the beginning. I have often observed that the inner circles of highly successful people are rarely populated with new contacts made after they received national media coverage. The people in their tribe, after their "big break", are the people who were there from the start. They are usually genuine colleagues who expected nothing in return, but have added value along the way.

As we saw earlier, this is how I met Brandon T. Adams. When I stumbled across his crowdfunding campaign for the Young Entrepreneur Convention, I realized that this was the beginning of a potentially groundbreaking project. Brandon and his team built their campaign to attract engagement. Luck is a two-sided coin. Brandon's crowdfunding page and online efforts were designed to attract someone like myself and I am always on the lookout for new projects that align with my values. One side of this seemingly lucky coin was designed to attract someone and the other side open to opportunities wherever they may be found. The circumstances around our meeting are undeniably providential, but since then we have intentionally nurtured the friendship.

There are numerous people with vision and strong ideas who are longing to connect with the right audience. Finding your authentic tribe takes a bit of effort but, if you are willing to devote the time to identify the voices calling out to your inner passions, you may stumble upon new relationships that are just right for you. The people you hope to meet want to be found and have been trying to get your attention. Listening may just be the most effective tool in our relational toolbox.

How to Meet People: Throw Your Own Events

The most effective strategy for meeting a variety of diverse people with similar values and drive is to throw your own events. Events take on the personality, vision, values and energy of the organizing team. When you throw your own events, you become a magnet attracting likeminded people across various disciplines, having drawn them to your unique spin on a theme. One of the most powerful networking effects of throwing events is that you become the perceived influencer in the field in which the event lives. There is no need to fuss over the size of the first event. If you place the focus on providing as much value as you can within the framework of your mission, vision and values, then it will be a success no matter how small.

- What events could YOU throw in your field?
- What new energy and ideas could you bring to the table from your skillset and perspective in your industry?
- What value could you add to the lives and careers of the attendees?

The events I currently throw include speaking events, arts-related networking events, concerts, fundraisers, masterminds, food lover events, and start-up focused networking events. One of the ways to quickly grow the reach of your event is to partner with companies, influencers or organizations who have email lists that would find value in the content. You can ask them to be a marketing sponsor for your event, which could include advertising the event to their network. This is one of the fastest ways to grow interest in a new event. If your event goes well or even appears innovative, then people in the city and your industry will begin reaching out to YOU for advice, making you offers, and quite possibly resulting in more incredible outcomes. The better you understand your event's target market, the more you can make informed decisions on who might be the best partners.

How to Meet People: The Cold Call Email

If you consider this book a springboard to your own creative ways to build relationships, you will be well on your way to discovering your unique take on this important skill of relational networking. We've discussed various methods for meeting people through events, but I would like to turn the discussion to a strategy that is often more daunting: *The Cold Call Email.*

While there are numerous relationships that can be built in person, there are many more that must happen virtually. The foremost question on everyone's mind, when beginning a correspondence with a stranger, is *How to write an email to which someone will respond?* Crafting a cold call email is a skill, not a talent. The indisputable element in the development of any skill is practice. We have all heard that practice makes perfect, but I would like to challenge that notion. If the building blocks of the desired skill you are learning are not sound, then your hours of practice will yield undesirable results. I believe that practice makes consistent. When over many years we flex a skillset, those actions become second nature. While this might sound positive, not all our second-nature abilities are promising. I can play a Brahms violin sonata because I've practiced the violin for over 10,000 hours, but I am unable to draw anything more than a stick figure model even though I have wielded a pencil since I was a young child. So, what kind of practice 'makes perfect'?

Perfect practice makes perfect

If your approach to cold call emails is informed by useful strategies, then the practice of these techniques will yield results that will improve upon use. I learned everything that I know about the principles for writing cold call emails from Derek Halpern. He is a marketing guru and the founder of Socialtriggers.com. The first thing that I learned is that two of the most common initial email mistakes include:

- Making the message all about YOU
- Sending the same universal message

It is understandable when writing to a stranger that you want to give them a convincing image of who you are, to persuade them to respond to you. In an age of decreasing attention spans and an increase in the sources vying for your attention, an introductory email which is all about you comes across as noise. Each new self-centered sentence causes the reader's interest to significantly diminish.

Generic emails, on the other hand, can be easily exposed and usually contain no information showing an authentic interest. Your dream contact will usually have no urgency to respond and your message will most likely be forgotten before it has been deleted. Earlier I mentioned the strategy of adding value to someone as a means of building a relationship. Sending a generic offer to help (i.e. "let me know how I can help you") makes the person you are writing responsible for thinking of how you, a stranger, can benefit their work. Many of the people we hope to connect with are busy and your email asking them to think of a way to collaborate with you, may easily be ignored.

At this point, I hope you're on the edge of your chair wondering about the alternative. The alternative to generic emails and emails that are all about you is writing an email built on a pyramid of incentives. Derek taught me that the higher ranking the target influencer is, the larger the incentive you want to offer. In the bestselling book *Freakonomics*, by Stephen Dubner and Steven Levitt, we learn that there are 3 types of incentives that can activate interest and lead to a response.

- Economic
- Social
- Moral

Simply put, writing from the perspective of an economic interest involves an offer of money, book sales, future deals and other financial reasons. The social incentive lives in the space of people's desire to fit in or be associated with an idea or other influencer who has equal or greater perceived prestige. The moral motivation to respond pulls at the heart strings and makes parallels to a greater good.

I spent a few weeks studying Derek's principles and then put them to the test. Here's an example letter I wrote to an author. I was surprised to receive a reply a few hours later.

(author's name has been removed for privacy)

Dear Mr. XXX,

I'm excited to write to you. As excited as some preteen writing Beyoncé or Justin Bieber. Thank-you for writing XXX. I think of your book now more like an encyclopedia as I endeavor to transform the lives of inner city youth through the audacious vehicle of a symphony Orchestra (check out our 1st concert).

I believe New England Music for social change teachers would love and eat up (your books). I think EVERYONE should know about these amazing resources!! Would you be interested in doing an hour and a half talk and Q and A about teaching and learning, as part of a professional development series I'm starting in 2014 for music for social change teachers all over New England? We'll also be able to end with a pitch for your books and sell them to attendees!!

We currently have world-renowned conductor and TED Speaker XXX on board and World Class violin teacher XXX. Would love to have you join this top tier group of speakers.

I know that your talk will have a profound impact on making the world a better place through the transformation of the teachers working with inner city youth!

I look forward to hearing back from you so I know whether to follow up or not. I started this professional development series as a way to promote innovative revolutionaries in the education space like you, so I hope you can join us in 2014.

Sincerely,

Can you spot which incentives I used in the letter? Writing a persuasive email takes time and a lot of trial and error. In the letter above, you will see my attempts to subtly employ the three incentives.

The first paragraph is short and expresses my real excitement to connect with the author. I write nothing about myself, even though it's tempting to try to impress the reader with the most impressive items from my resume; instead, I put the entire focus on the person with whom I'm hoping to make a connection.

At first glance it appears that my letter doesn't use the financial incentive, but if you look a little deeper you'll see it.

"I think everyone should know of these resources."

This short sentence hopes to trigger the author's desire to build and diversify his audience, which would lead to more book sales. I then follow up with a less subtle appeal to the financial incentive.

> *"We'll also be able to end with a pitch for your books and sell them to attendees!!"*

If you are unable to offer something that is clearly financial, you want to be mindful that the reader will be asking herself, 'What is in this for ME?' and you want your letter to make that clear.

The very next paragraph is short and sweet, going for the jugular and using the social incentive.

> *"We currently have world-renowned conductor and TED Speaker XXX on board and World Class violin teacher XXX. Would love to have you join this top tier group of speakers."*

People want to be associated with other people they consider to be in their social circle or higher. Being able to make this connection can be very useful. If you don't have other heavyweights associated with your project, you may mention the other influential stakeholders you hope to get involved in your endeavor as an enticement.

I then make a swift move to the moral incentive.

"I know that your talk will have a profound impact on making the world a better place through the transformation of the teachers working with inner city youth!"

Every influencer is putting out content to have some effect on the world. If you can tap into what that effect might be and provide a relevant way in which your collaboration complements their goals, this will be a powerful trigger.

Before I close the letter, I make a final appeal using the social incentive.

I started this professional development series as a way to ***promote innovative revolutionaries*** *in the education space* ***like you***.

I hit the send button and was excited to receive a swift reply. You can read his answer below.

The response email:

Dear David,

Thanks for sending the (terrific) video and the invitation.

> I'm completely intrigued, and I'd love to hear more. What dates do you have in mind?
>
> Thanks,
>
> XXX

The incentives worked! I probably spent more than a few hours writing this letter based on Derek's principles and template – and the result was worth it. His reply is short and, more importantly, sweet! Most influencers or other highly sought-after leaders are inundated with generic letters that don't stand out. If you take the time to study who you are writing to and wrestle with the best way to use the three incentives, then I believe you will be surprised by your ability to connect with people seemingly out of reach.

I challenge you to try constructing your own letter and then send it. When you do, write me a note letting me know what strategies worked for you!

CHAPTER
5

FOLLOW UP: COME TO MIND

THE CONCEPTS ON the next few pages are far more important than the strategies regarding how and where to meet people. The number one most neglected aspect of relationship-building is the art of cultivation. Most people I know have stacks of business cards from events they went to years ago. They are waiting for the perfect moment to finally respond. The truth is, the longer you wait to reply, the more that relationship loses value exponentially. Within a matter of time, the reasons why you wanted to connect may now be irrelevant and the person you were eager to connect with may no longer remember you.

So how do you stay in the mind of people that you've met?

Staying in the mind of people in your network is a concept I call *Come to mind*. The leading way to stay in people's mind is by having a follow-up strategy. Follow-up strategies work remarkably well because they are rarely utilized, therefore immediately set you apart to be remembered.

Here are five strategies to help you.

Act Immediately

My memory tends to be more like a sieve than a tightly-woven basket. When I go to events and meet various people, it is difficult for me to remember the details of the people that I've met. My memory is often triggered if the company name or the job title on the business card involves an arena of service that I have needed. This has led me to strategy number one, which is *Act Immediately*. Shortly after getting a business card, I jot notes on the back of the card recalling the details of the conversation and any other pertinent specifics that will make following up more advantageous.

Connect Virtually

When I return home from an event, I take the time to connect virtually with people I have met using professional and personal social media platforms. While I am decidedly professional on each of my social media outlets, I use them in separate ways and think of them like an old-school rolodex. I take cues from the conversation to determine which would be the best fit. In my head, I liken each platform to a particular social setting.

LinkedIn is the boardroom

Twitter is like a cocktail party

Facebook is my living room

Instagram is that coffee table book in the living room

Snapchat is my inner sanctum or bedroom

Most people I meet will ask if they can connect on LinkedIn. When the platform is chosen for me, this step is easier. But a few times people might ask to be added on a platform that is bit more personal than I would like, and in that case, I tactfully suggest another social medium. There are some people you would prefer to talk to at a cocktail party but would rather not chat with in your living room. You want to make your choice based on which platform will best nurture that relationship. I would suggest developing a unique style for each platform based on their distinctive strengths. I find that I am a bit more experimental on Snapchat, therefore I am more careful of whom I choose to add there. Adding people on several platforms will give them a better picture of your values and work ethic, while also giving you more opportunities to *come to mind.*

Categorize for the Future

Whenever I meet someone, and we decide to exchange cards to facilitate future professional conversations, I make sure to add them to one of my curated email lists on my CRM (Customer Relationship Management) of choice: MailChimp. I have numerous lists for my current and future projects, as well as for every event I have ever thrown or hope to throw in the future. Based on the intersection of our interests, I decide on the best list(s) to add them to. I do this immediately because it frees me from having to remember how every single person I meet is uniquely connected to one of my many interests and projects. For example, if someone is fired up about inner city youth getting access to music education and have expressed a desire to come to one of our shows, I'll add them to our concert list. When we have a concert, they will get a personal email from me inviting them, so that I don't have to remember each and every person that wanted this information.

My lists encompass my array of interests and you may have one or many lists that correspond to your unique needs. I often have ideas for future projects and have lists for these as well. I once had an idea for an event three years before I launched it and, over those years, I slowly added people who I thought would be interested. When the event finally materialized, I had a mailing list of a few hundred people and the event was a success!

My lists fall into several categories. Here are a few of the groupings:

- Arts-based networking events
- Concerts
- Nonprofit Newsletter
- Personal Newsletter
- Young Professionals event
- Future books I hope to write

While I do not completely advise that you add people to lists they have not asked to join, I am not too worried about this strategy because people can always choose to unsubscribe from the list.

When throwing events, it is very helpful to use a ticketing source that collects attendee information, even if the event is free. If you end up having a smaller turnout than you wanted and have no access to the few people that came, you will have to start from scratch the next time you hope to build an audience for your work. If you commit to this strategy over time, you will grow a robust and valuable mailing list.

If I do not take the time on the night of the event to go through these steps, I am not very likely to ever nurture that relationship. I tell myself that, if I do not think I have time to go through these steps that night, then I should not have gone to the event in the first place.

Categorize for the Future: Relationship Document

The tangible value of mutually beneficial relationships cannot be simply measured. Their benefits spread deep, very much like the roots of a well-watered tree. What you gain from relationships far outvalues the upfront work it takes to initiate them.

If your memory is as malleable as mine, you might wonder how you can keep people from falling through the cracks. Following up is the most important aspect of relational networking. Because of this, we need more tools to keep key relationships fresh in OUR mind and a way for YOU to be remembered.

Over the years, I have created a relationship document in order to organize information about some of the more significant people that I have met. The spreadsheet is systematized by a few major headings.

Super Connectors: People I have met who love connecting people

Good Friends: Personal friends and business contacts that have turned into personal friendships

Event Specific: People I have met at specific events and conferences

City Specific: Significant people I have met in one city or country

Super connectors are those people who not only love connecting people but are damn good at it. They have a genuine love for people and are magnets for diverse people from all walks of life and in countless industries. This is the first tab in my relationship document, because these are the people who care the most about helping others. You may overhear one of their conversations sounding like this, "You should meet so and so. Let's grab coffee sometime and I'll introduce you."

I keep a tab for **good friends** because, the busier you get, the harder it may become to nurture relationships with our personal friends outside of work. Having this tab acts like a nudge to help me to be mindful of these relationships and to give them the attention they deserve.

Have you ever thought, 'who were those people I met at that conference last year?' Having a tab that lists the people that I meet at a specific event helps to solve that dilemma. Each event has its own tab.

As an avid traveler, I am often in cities around the world and value meaningful relationships far above monuments. When meeting so many people, it can be hard to remember all the people I have met in different cities. Having a tab that is city **specific** or **country specific** helps. This past summer I had the honor of working at *Lean Start*, Cyprus's first incubator for high school students. While there, I created a tab for the country of Cyprus and included the contact information of people from each city I visited. I may return in the future, therefore, having this information within reach will be a great guide as I seek to nurture specific relationships.

In each tab there is room for meaningful information, beyond the basics of name and contact info. These details include:

Passions: What is this person most passionate about?

Before I die: What is one thing this person wants to accomplish before they die?

Why: Why have I added them on that particular list? Who introduced me to them?

Who: Who are people that I would like to connect them with? Who would they like to connect me with?

Value: What value can I bring to their work?

Now this seems like a lot of work, but every tab doesn't have to include all the details above. Consider this document a work in progress. As you get to know each person, *over time,* you will fill in the information as it emerges in the relationship. Also, this is not a definitive list, so you should feel free to include areas important to you!

Categorize for the Future: The Personal Touch

After meeting someone, I send them a personal email thanking them for the conversation, while subtly recapping what we talked about. I try to include as much detail as possible, so that the email will act as a digital sticky note for future reference. I will recount what I may have enjoyed and what I learned from the interaction. I will also include any action items that require a follow-up.

Categorize for the Future: Schedule all Future Correspondence

The last step in this process is to schedule all future correspondence. I will first pick a date in the future to write a follow-up message. I use Google calendar because you can choose the "repeat" event option to spread the reminder over a certain period. The nature of the connection and their perceived busyness will determine the frequency of the communication. If I intend to write someone only once or twice a year, I will set the calendar reminder for once every 26 or 52 weeks. Most of us are inundated with emails, therefore writing to someone less won't clog their inbox and can be enough for you to stay on their mind. If the collaboration is more imminent, I may set the reminder for every few weeks. When the reminder comes up, I treat it as a scheduled meeting and make the time to send a short message.

I've learned from social media experts the importance of staying active online. This is one of the premier ways to stay on people's mind. Using the platforms that fit your style can be a great vehicle to nurturing ongoing relationships. Those who gain the most value from their social media presence will post valuable content every day. If you have taken the time to follow-up in a thoughtful way and post quality content online on a regular basis, you WILL come to mind when an opportunity fit becomes available. Posting quality content is more important than daily postings and having a systematic strategy regarding your frequency drives engagement.

The existence of this book is an applicable case study. We have all seen the social media vacation photos that make us wish we were somewhere else. What if these albums could not only be fun but strategic? This past summer, I bought a one-way ticket to Barcelona. I challenged myself to figure out how to make enough money, while playing violin on the streets of Europe, for a return ticket to Boston. I have learned some the most life-changing lessons through challenging circumstances. I believe this trip was a gift from God and was gifted to me to share with others. I have had numerous trips of a lifetime in Europe, which are always unpredictable adventures filled with meaningful conversations and unbelievable tales. I decided to share my most inspiring encounters in as much detail as I could recall. The circumstances that came my way and my response allowed me to share my personality, values and worldview in a new and more personal way. Every post was well thought out and the main desire was to cultivate an intimate relationship with hundreds of people, staying on their mind, while keeping them on the edge of their seat with the next true tale.

In the middle of my summer adventure, I received a message on Facebook from my friend Brandon T. Adams, asking for a Skype meeting. I sat in a café, on an island in Croatia, with my computer opened to Skype. I was sent to this island by a 15-year-old in Slovenia who wanted to contribute to my trip, so I asked him to decide which country would be my next destination. Brandon had been following my adventure online while he was organizing an event in Iowa. He wanted someone to speak at his weekend mastermind about "How to build professional relationships with anyone you meet." My regular snapshots of my encounters put me in a position to come to mind as a potential guest speaker. I accepted the invitation and spent the rest of my trip preparing a three-hour workshop on relationships. That workshop has turned into this book.

CONCLUSION

This book is solely a list of ingredients and you are the master chef. If you create your own recipe using these principles, then you are more likely to come to mind when someone in your network has a perfect project for you. The tricky part is being able to see the opportunity as an opportunity. What emerges for you will not be comparable to what has become available for me, but that should not negate its worth. If you compare yourself to a colleague, you only hinder yourself from seeing the numerous opportunities that YOU are being offered. There are many reasons to listen to the seemingly rational voice in your head telling you to say no to those prospects, but I have noticed that the people who appear to have "luck" on their side, say yes far more often.

I never assume that an opportunity I am given will ever be offered again. My opportunities look very different than my colleagues, but they're mine. Embrace the fact that wherever life has placed you, therein lies YOUR opportunity. I keep my eyes wide open for these hidden gems and consider them the fortuitous fruit of showing up. If you don't show up, you deny yourself the myriad of possibilities that can emerge from a single convening.

Want to know how to meet the perfect person who will open the door to your lifelong dreams? The simple yet complex answer is that you must become that person. If you meet people with the purpose of listening to their story, you will no doubt hear a story you've never heard before that may change your perspective. If you spend less time trying to find the perfect super-connector and more time becoming that connector, you will be able to associate with almost anyone you meet. Why? Because if you add value to the people you meet, you will be the person THEY are looking for. If your values align, it may be the beginning of an amazing adventure.

Your unique personality, interests and values can create a natural bridge to a wide range of people. When the connection is a natural fit, you will not have to compete for attention but will only have to spend the necessary time to follow up and stay connected. Remembering that relationships are not about what you can get but what you can offer is the secret to relationship building.

Relationships are an important key to what makes life significant. They are not about being savvy enough to figure out who can get you the furthest. They are instead, a conduit for you to provide value and real support to people whose success you genuinely care about. When you connect on the deepest level of values and mission, the fruit of these relationships will not only make your life more meaningful, but will open a world of opportunity beyond your wildest imagination. If none of this happens for you, the support you give to others will impact the future of the world, for the better. Now put this book down; there are people waiting for YOU to show up.

Did you enjoy this book?

I'd be honored if you could share your thoughts and post a quick review on Amazon!

ABOUT THE AUTHOR

David France is an international performer and an innovative educator. He is currently the founder and Executive Director of Revolution of Hope, a music for social change non-profit in Boston. He was recently named a Top 100 Most Influential Person of Color in Boston and a Top 40 Urban Innovator Under 40 in the United States. In 2009 he became the Concertmaster of the first orchestra auditioned on the internet, The YouTube Symphony. He has performed with legendary musicians such as Kenny Rogers, Josh Groban, and Quincy Jones. He has been featured by the *Associated Press, The New York Times, Time Magazine, NBC Nightly News*, and BBC Radio. As a keynote speaker he has spoken at The Harvard Kennedy School, the Babson Entrepreneurship Forum, Lean Gap, and Endevrr a High School Entrepreneurship program at UPENN where he was also a mentor. He is the founder of Ziryab Ventures a think tank for young entrepreneurs and is an Associate producer on the Emmy Nominated TV show *Ambitious*

Adventures. When he is not juggling multiple projects, you can find him biking the streets of Boston, cooking delicious meals after midnight, and traveling the world with no money. He believes that joy in this life is maximized when you *Give Your Life Away.*

www.davidfranceviolin.com

Bonus Resources

Stories from the Cutting Room Floor

Book Related Resources

- Relationship Management Spreadsheet
- Relational Networking Checklist

Coaching

- Crowdfunding
- Business Development
- Project Management
- Social Media
- Marketing
- Weight Loss
- String Pedagogy
- Violin Lessons

Booking

- Speaking
- Podcasts

- Workshops
- Guest Blog
- Radio & TV
- Book Tour
- Press inquiries

Show up!

Want to collaborate with David France on YOUR project idea. Get a free 15 min. skype chat to discuss the details.

Check out these exciting Bonus items here!

www.davidfranceviolin.com/showupbonus

Made in the USA
Columbia, SC
05 March 2018